Math All Around
Subtraction at School

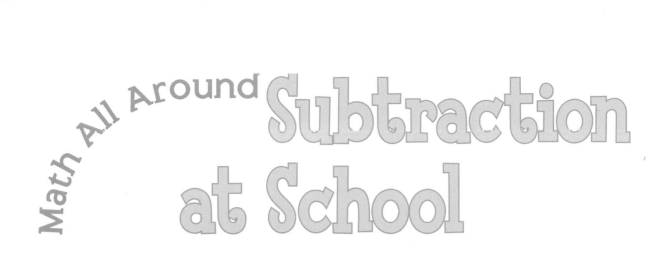

Jennifer Rozines Roy and Gregory Roy

 **Marshall Cavendish**
Benchmark
New York

Do you think **subtraction** is just for math class? You can use subtraction throughout the school day!

Subtraction is used to take away. When you subtract, you find a missing part.

That's the school bell! Time to start the day and subtract away!

First thing in the morning, your teacher takes attendance. There are seventeen students total in your class. Who is here today? Who is missing?

Two kids are out sick. One is away on vacation. That makes three absent.

Let's find out how many kids are here today on this number line.

There are fourteen students in class today.
Ready for more subtraction action? Let's go!

Take out a book and get comfortable. It's time to read. You and your friend are both reading the same book.

Your friend has read thirty pages. You have read only twenty so far. How many pages do you need to read to catch up with your friend?

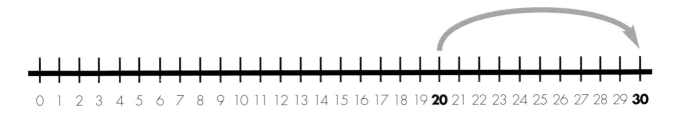

0 1 2 3 4 5 6 7 8 9 10 11 12 13 14 15 16 17 18 19 **20** 21 22 23 24 25 26 27 28 29 **30**

You can figure out the number of pages by using subtraction or you can count up. You need to read ten more pages to get to the same page as your friend. But don't hurry. You can both enjoy your books at your own speed. It's free reading—not speeding!

After reading, it's time to write stories. Two of the pencils in your pencil box are old and short, but one is new and sharpened.

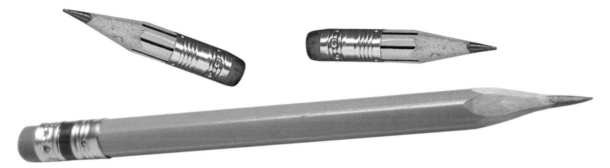

3 pencils total – **2** old pencils = **1** new pencil

A subtraction fact is made up of numbers, a **minus sign** and an **equal sign**. The minus sign means "take away."

If you have three pencils, and take away the two that are worn down, you have one good pencil left. You can read the subtraction fact as, "Three minus two equals one."

Maybe you can write a story about a subtraction superhero!

Grab your sneakers. It's time for gym class.
Today you're playing basketball. Throw the ball
up and into the net!

After your first great shot, you throw six misses in a row. Keep trying!

Swish! Another one through the hoop!

Swish! And another!

Air ball! Whoops. That was your last shot of the day.

Let's see:

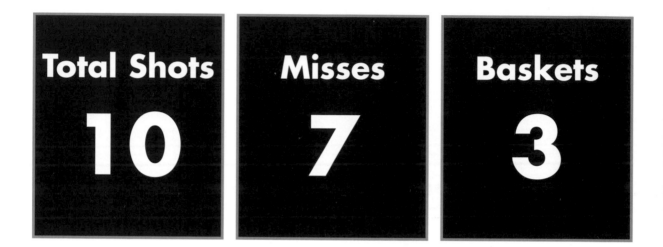

We can make subtraction facts from these numbers. A subtraction fact can be written in a line across, or in a column. The first number is the number you are taking away from.

How many baskets?

10 − 7 = 3

$$\begin{array}{r} 10 \\ -\ 7 \\ \hline 3 \end{array}$$

←*(this line means "equals")*

How many misses?

10 − 3 = 7

$$\begin{array}{r} 10 \\ -\ 3 \\ \hline 7 \end{array}$$

And how much fun doing sports subtraction? Lots and lots, of course!

Stop at the water fountain for a drink. Boy, gym class really makes you thirsty!

There are two fountains in this hall, so two students can drink at a time. You and your friend reach the fountains first. Everybody else is waiting for their turn.

The greater number in a subtraction problem is called the **minuend**. This is the number from which you subtract.

The number you subtract is the **subtrahend**.

minuend	**14**	students in class
subtrahend	**– 2**	students drinking
	12	thirsty students

It's time for computer class. There are eighteen computers in the lab. Two are not working today. Will there still be enough computers for each student?

No problem! There are sixteen computers for fourteen students.

The answer in a subtraction problem is called the **difference**. The difference between **18** and **2** is **16**.

Grumble, grumble. That's the sound of a hungry student's belly. Let's go to the cafeteria. What's for lunch today?

Yum! First you gobble down half of your sandwich. That leaves one half.

2 halves − **1** half = **1** half

Munch, munch. You're so hungry, you quickly eat the rest.

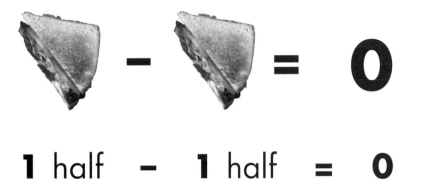

1 half **–** **1** half **=** **0**

No more sandwich. When a number is subtracted from itself, the difference is zero.

Take out the cherries. Eat all fourteen of them. *Chew, chew.* All gone.

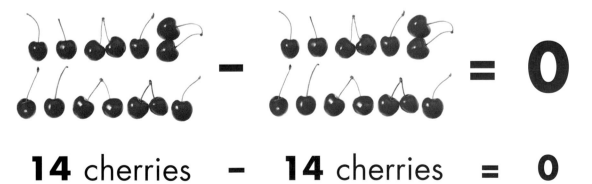

14 cherries **–** **14** cherries **=** **0**

Now look at your milk cartons. You're not really thirsty after drinking all that water at the fountain. You decide to save them for later.

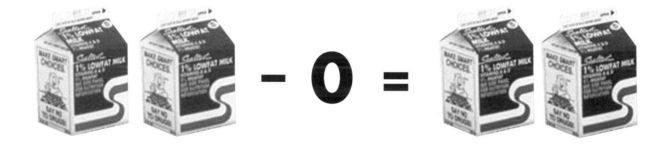

2 milk cartons   **–**   **0** milk cartons used   **=**   **2** milk cartons left

When zero is subtracted from a number, the difference is that number.

That's a lot of zeroes you used subtracting in the lunchroom today. Hey, your friend gives you a doughnut. That's so nice, and look—another zero!

Recess! Run outside toward the swing set. The fastest kids get their turn to swing first.

There are two swings and six kids who want to swing.

$$6 - 2 = 4$$

The difference is four. Today, you don't make it in time. You and three other kids will have to wait.

Three of the girls go off to jump rope. That leaves you.

4 − 3 = 1

That's okay. The soccer game needs another player!

Your friend passes you the ball. You are headed for the goal when… *ow!* You fall down hard. Subtract one hurt player from the game.

You walk to the nurse's office. The nurse takes a look and says you have a small bump. She gives you an ice pack to hold against your head. You'll be fine soon.

Then the nurse asks you to help her count bandages while you're there.

The bandages come thirty-two in a box. You count twenty-one left inside. How many have been used?

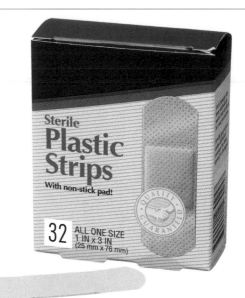

$$3\mathbf{2}$$ *(subtract the ones)*
$$-2\mathbf{1}$$
$$\overline{\quad\mathbf{1}\quad}$$

$$\mathbf{3}2$$ *(then subtract the tens)*
$$-\mathbf{2}1$$
$$\overline{\mathbf{1}1}$$

When you subtract larger numbers, you subtract from right to left, beginning with the ones place. Eleven bandages were used from that box.

The nurse smiles. If you can subtract that well, your head must be okay! Back to class.

Glossary

difference—The answer in a subtraction problem.

equal sign—A sign used in math to show an equal, or same, amount.

minuend—The number from which you subtract.

minus sign—A sign used in math to show subtraction.

subtraction—A math operation that tells you how much greater one number is than another.

subtrahend—The number you subtract.

Read More

Ajmera, Maya and John Ivanko, *Back to School*, Massachusetts: Charlesbridge, 2001.

Caron, Lucille, and Philip M. St. Jacques, *Addition and Subtraction*. Berkeley Heights, NJ: Enslow, 2001.

Leedy, Loreen, *Subtraction Action*. New York: Holiday House, 2000.

Scholastic Explains Math Homework. New York: Scholastic, 1998.

Web Sites

Flashcards for Kids
http://edu4kids.com/math

The Math Forum: Ask Dr. Math
http://mathforum.com/dr.math

Index

Page numbers in **boldface** are illustrations.

About the Authors

Jennifer Rozines Roy is the author of more than twenty books. A former Gifted and Talented teacher, she holds degrees in psychology and elementary education.

Gregory Roy is a civil engineer who has co-authored several books with his wife. The Roys live in upstate New York with their son Adam.

Marshall Cavendish Benchmark
99 White Plains Road
Tarrytown, New York 10591-9001
www.marshallcavendish.us

Library of Congress Cataloging-in-Publication Data

Roy, Jennifer Rozines, 1967-
Subtraction at school / by Jennifer Rozines Roy and Gregory Roy.
p. cm. — (Math all around)
Summary: "Reinforces both subtraction and reading skills, stimulates critical thinking, and
provides students with an understanding of math in the real world"—Provided by publisher.
Includes bibliographical references and index.
ISBN 0-7614-2003-7
1. Subtraction—Juvenile literature. 2. Arithmetic—Juvenile literature. 3. Critical thinking—Juvenile literature.
I. Roy, Gregory. II. Title. III. Series.
QA115.R69 2005
513.2'12—dc22
2005005784

Photo Research by Anne Burns Images

Cover Photo by *Corbis*/Macduff Everton

The photographs in this book are used with the permission and through the courtesy of:
SuperStock: pp. 1, 24, 25, 27 age fotostock; p. 6 Anton Vengo; p. 8 t r l Den Reader; pp. 8 b, 23 SuperStock; p. 9 Kevin Radford;
p. 21 Comstock. *Corbis*: p. 2 Tom & Dee Ann McCarthy; p. 4 Jim Cummins; p. 5 Chris Collins; pp. 10, 11 Duomo;
p. 14 LWA-Dann Tardif; p. 16 Ed Bock; p. 17 John Madere; p. 18 t Charles Gupton; pp. 18 b, 19 t, 19 b, 26 Royalty Free;
p. 20 Owen Franken; p. 22 Karl Weatherly.

Series design by Virginia Pope

Printed in Malaysia
1 3 5 6 4 2